Bruce Lee

Terry Barber

ENTERTAINERS

Bruce Lee is published by
Grass Roots Press, a division of Literacy Services of Canada Ltd.

www.grassrootsbooks.net

ACKNOWLEDGEMENTS

We acknowledge the financial support of the
Government of Canada for our publishing activities.   **Canadä**

Produced with the assistance of
the Government of Alberta through the
Alberta Multimedia Development Fund.   *Alberta*

Editor: Dr. Pat Campbell
Image research: Dr. Pat Campbell
Book design: Lara Minja

Library and Archives Canada Cataloguing in Publication

Barber, Terry, date, author
  Bruce Lee / Terry Barber.

(Entertainers)

ISBN 978–1–77153–103–0 (softcover)

   1. Readers for new literates. 2. Lee, Bruce, 1940-1973. 3. Martial artists—United States—Biography. 4. Actors—United States--Biography. 5. Motion picture actors and actresses—United States—Biography. 6. Biographies. I. Title.

PE1126.N43B3445 2017   428.6'2   C2017–904625–X

Printed in Canada

Contents

Bruce eats lunch with friends.

Inner Power

Bruce meets friends in a nice restaurant. They order lunch. The waiter is rude to Bruce. The waiter is rude to Bruce again. Bruce just smiles. Bruce won't let a rude waiter spoil his day.

Bruce is in control of his emotions.

Inner Power

Bruce is a **martial artist.** To some, he is the greatest martial artist of all time. Bruce could say something rude to the waiter. Bruce could hurt the rude waiter. But Bruce won't. Being a martial artist means more than kicks and punches.

Bruce believes you learn how to fight so you don't have to fight.

Bruce walks away from the table.

Inner Power

Bruce's approach to life is simple. He controls his thoughts. He controls his actions. What can Bruce gain by hurting the waiter with words or blows? Bruce has no need to show off his skills. Bruce is happy to walk away.

Bruce Lee and his mother, brothers, and sisters.

Early Years

Bruce is born in 1940. Bruce is born in San Francisco. His parents are from Hong Kong. His father, Lee Hoi-chuen, is an actor. His mother, Grace Ho, is from a rich family. Bruce has two brothers and two sisters.

Bruce is born in the **Year of the Dragon**.

A street in Hong Kong.
1941

Early Years

When Bruce is still a baby, the family moves back to Hong Kong. His family lives in Kowloon. As a young boy, Bruce works as an actor. He stars in more than 20 movies. Bruce also likes to dance. Bruce wins contests as a dancer.

Bruce stars in his first film at the age of three months.

13

Yip Man and Bruce Lee.

Early Years

At school, the boys bully Bruce. The boys think Bruce is a **sissy** because he acts. Bruce wants to defend himself. Bruce studies **Wing Chun** when he is 16 years old. Bruce joins a gang and gets into street fights. The police know about Bruce.

Yip Man teaches Wing Chun to Bruce.

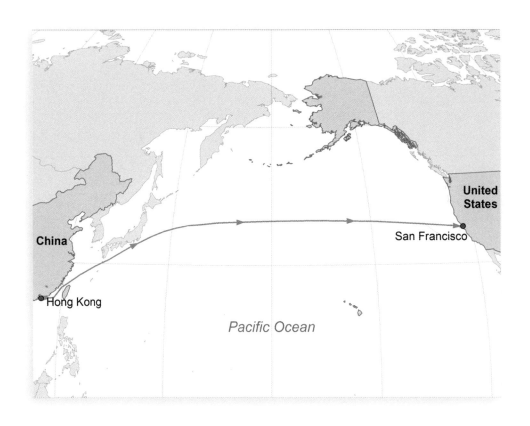

At age 18, Bruce travels by ship to San Francisco.

A New Life

Bruce's parents want him to stay out of trouble. They want Bruce to stay out of jail. Bruce's parents send him back to San Francisco. There, Bruce lives with his older sister. Bruce works in a restaurant.

Bruce works at the Ruby Chow restaurant.

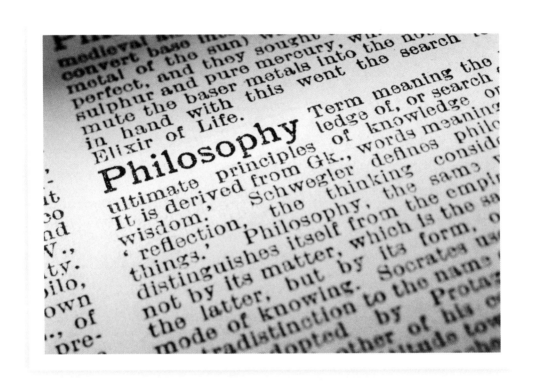

Philosophy is the study of the meaning of life.

A New Life

Bruce goes to university in 1961. He teaches martial arts to pay his bills. Bruce studies **philosophy**. Bruce loves to study philosophy. He reads book after book about philosophy. Bruce finds a love he follows all his life.

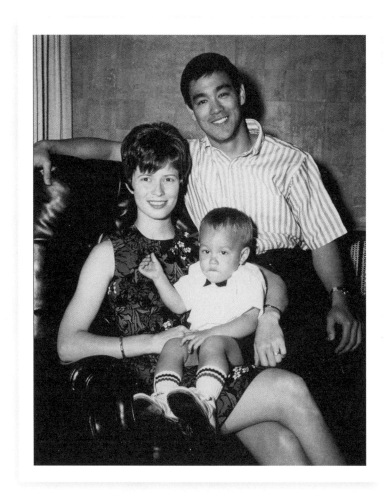

Bruce, Linda, and their son Brandon.

A New Life

In university, Bruce finds an even deeper love. Bruce meets Linda. She is a student in his martial arts class. Soon, Linda and Bruce go out on dates. In 1964, they become husband and wife.

Bruce and Linda have two children.

A martial arts class.

The Teacher

Bruce leaves university. Bruce wants to teach martial arts full time. He believes most students take classes to become street fighters. But most students are taught to swing wide with kicks and punches. Those types of moves won't win a street fight.

Bruce opens three martial arts studios.

Students practise **kung fu**.

The Teacher

Bruce wants to change how martial arts is taught. Dance is taught step by step. Martial arts are often taught the same way. Bruce thinks martial arts should be taught like a street fight. Short, quick moves win a street fight.

Bruce teaches students how to kick.

The Teacher

Being able to kick in the right way is important. Being able to punch in the right way is important. But a person needs more than those skills. Bruce believes people must train their bodies *and* their minds.

Bruce likes to balance thinking with doing.

The Teacher

Many other martial artists dislike
Bruce. They say, "You are too young
to teach a martial art. You should not
teach martial arts to non-Chinese."
But Bruce does not care what others
say or think. Bruce is his own person.

Bruce Lee says,
"As you think, so shall you become."

The Thinker

People must train their minds to be open. People must train their minds to be calm.

Bruce believes in balance. Bruce likes to balance thinking time with doing time.

Bruce also believes that people should be like water.

Bruce believes people should be like water.

The Thinker

Bruce says: "Empty your mind, be formless. Shapeless like water. Now you put water into a cup, it becomes the cup. You put water into a bottle, it becomes the bottle. You put it in a teapot, it becomes the teapot."

Bruce Lee fights crime in *The Green Hornet*.

The Actor

It is 1967. Bruce still teaches and he starts to act again. Bruce is an actor in *The Green Hornet*. Bruce fights crime in this TV show.

People in Hong Kong watch this show. Bruce becomes famous in Hong Kong.

The Green Hornet lasts for only one season.

A *Fists of Fury* poster.
1972

The Actor

Bruce wants to act on the big screen. But Hollywood isn't ready for an Asian leading man. Bruce returns to Hong Kong in 1971. In Hong Kong, Bruce makes a movie. Bruce calls the movie *Fists of Fury*.

Fists of Fury is a box-office hit.

Bruce Lee's star is on a famous street in Hollywood.

The Actor

By 1972, Hollywood sees that Bruce is a star. Hollywood asks Bruce to act in a movie. Bruce opens the door for other Asian actors. Asian directors get jobs. Asian stuntmen get jobs. Bruce helps other Asians reach their goals.

Bruce Lee is known as the King of Kung Fu.

Bruce likes to write movie scripts.

The Actor

Bruce acts in many movies. He does his own stunts in movies. Bruce wants his movies to make people think. People learn values from Bruce's movies.

Bruce is more than an actor. Bruce directs movies. Bruce produces movies. Bruce writes movie scripts.

A martial arts school in Japan.

The Star Still Shines

Bruce makes martial arts popular. Martial arts schools open around the world. Many other actors star in martial arts movies. Every movie wants a star like Bruce Lee. But there is only one Bruce Lee.

A Bruce Lee lookalike.

Bruce Lee is buried in Seattle, Washington.

The Star Still Shines

Bruce Lee dies in 1973. He is only 32 years old. He leaves behind his wife, Linda. He leaves behind two small children. Bruce leaves behind books and movies, which people still enjoy. The world misses Bruce Lee and his teachings.

Bruce dies from a reaction to pain medicine.

Glossary

kung fu: a form of combat and self-defence, using feet and hands.

martial artist: a person who practises a martial art such as kung fu or judo.

philosophy: the study of ideas and the meaning of life.

sissy: a negative name for a boy who likes things girls usually like.

Wing Chun: a type of kung fu.

Year of the Dragon: The Dragon is the fifth of the 12 Chinese zodiac animals. Years of the Dragon include 1940, 1952, 1964, 1976, 1988, 2000, 2012, and 2024.

Talking About the Book

What did you learn about Bruce Lee?

In your own words, describe Bruce's approach
to life.

Bruce believes in balance. What does this mean?

Why did Bruce want to learn kung fu?
Do you think others want to learn kung fu
for the same reason?

Bruce says, "As you think, so shall you become."
What do you think this means?

Picture Credits